SPYCRAFT

HOW TO BE THE BEST
SECRET AGENT EVER

Buster Books

Written by Martin Oliver
Illustrated by Simon Ecob
Edited by Rachel Carter and Imogen Williams
Designed by Barbara Ward
Cover design by John Bigwood
With thanks to Sally Pilkington and Anton Dalby

The publisher and the author disclaim all liability, as far as is legally
permitted, for accidents or injuries or loss of any nature that may
occur as a result of the use or misuse of the information and guidance
given in this book. Above all, exercise common sense, particularly
when fire or sharp objects are involved, and follow at all times safety
precautions and advice from responsible adults. That said, it is fun
to learn new skills, and they may one day be useful.

First published in Great Britain in 2018 by Buster Books,
an imprint of Michael O'Mara Books Limited,
9 Lion Yard, Tremadoc Road, London SW4 7NQ

 www.busterbooks.co.uk   Buster Children's Books   @BusterBooks

Material in this book previously appeared in *The Boys' Book of Spycraft*

Every reasonable effort has been made to acknowledge all copyright holders.
Any errors or omissions that may have occurred are inadvertent, and anyone
with any copyright queries is invited to write to the publishers, so that a full
acknowledgement may be included in subsequent editions of this work.

A CIP catalogue record for this book is available from the British Library.

ISBN: 978–1–78055–510–2

1 3 5 7 9 10 8 6 4 2

This book was printed in January 2018 by 1010 Printing International Ltd, 1010 Avenue,
Xia Nan Industrial District, Yuan Zhou Town, Bo Luo County, Hui Zhou City,
Guang Dong Province, China.

INTRODUCTION

This book contains all the skills you'll need to become the world's best secret agent. You'll learn everything from how to set up your spy ring and headquarters, to cracking codes and tailing suspects.

When you've read this book from start to finish, sign the certificate at the back of the book to show off your new know-how skills.

SAFE SPYING

The hints and tips in this book are intended for practice purposes only. Under no circumstances should you ever attempt any exercise that would put yourself or others in any danger in real life.

We urge you, at all times, to make yourself aware of, and obey, all laws, regulations and local by-laws, and respect all rights, including the rights of property owners. Always respect other people's privacy and remember to ask a responsible adult for assistance and take their advice whenever necessary.

CONTENTS

HOW TO ...
SET UP
A SPY RING

Although some spies prefer to work solo, it's a lot more fun to develop your headquarters, plan operations and pass messages with a group of friends. What you need to do is set up your own 'spy ring'. A spy ring is an undercover organization run by a 'spy master' along with several 'field agents' and a 'go-between'. Read on to find out more about these roles and how to recruit friends into your organization.

SPY MASTER

The person who sets up a spy ring is called the spy master. This is the most important role in a spy ring — so this is a job for you. The spy master is the person who decides on missions and strategy, and directs operations. A spy master's identity must be kept secret at all times.

FIELD AGENTS

Next there are field agents — spies who are out and about carrying out missions. A field agent does the exciting and difficult jobs, such as staking out suspects, passing on information, and mounting surveillance operations.

GO-BETWEEN

The final person in a spy ring is the go-between, who passes communications between the spy master and the field agents. The go-between is a level above a field agent, because they must be capable of acting as an active spy as well as being an excellent communicator.

STEP ONE

Your first step as spy master is to choose a suitable go-between. Pick someone you trust, but try not to be too obvious by picking your best friend — that could easily blow your cover.

Approach your potential go-between and discuss the idea of a spy ring. Don't identify yourself as the spy master. Just casually mention that you've heard that someone is setting up a secret club that sounds like it might be fun. Gauge your friend's reaction — if they seem interested, describe the role of the go-between. Why not say that you'd love to be chosen for that role? This helps to cover your identity as spy master, or as someone already involved in the ring at all.

STEP TWO

If a friend would like the job of go-between, wait a few days, then tell them you have been told to give them the task of recruiting up to four field agents. You could even allow yourself to be recruited, so that you have the fun of being a field agent while also protecting your real identity as the spy master.

THE RULES

Now it's time to get to grips with a few key rules of a spy ring:

- Keep the numbers in your spy ring to between four and six. If too many people are involved, you increase the risk of discovery.

- Any communication between the members of the ring should be in code (you will find a variety of suitable codes in this book).

- Make sure that during a mission all your agents are not working together at any one time. If you are discovered together, your spy ring can be blown wide open in just one moment. Operate in twos and threes.

- Ideally, as spy master, you should be the only one to know the identity of all the members of the ring and their roles. This way, if an agent is discovered and interrogated, they will not put your entire operation in jeopardy by naming other operatives. However, this won't be much fun for your friends and will make meetings very hard, so you will probably have to break this rule!

HOW TO ...

SET UP YOUR HEADQUARTERS

You've probably noticed that in spy films and books the characters are often multi-millionaires, with a secret cave or hideaway as their headquarters. If you don't have the funds for an underground cave complex, don't worry. With a little careful planning and foresight, you can create a highly-effective base for the espionage activities you'll soon be master-minding.

AWAY FROM PRYING EYES

A spy's headquarters should always be top-secret. If you have a garden you could build a camouflaged den (see pages 30-31). However, your bedroom, set up correctly, will make an excellent headquarters.

Here are the essential elements to include when setting up the perfect spy HQ in your bedroom:

- Your HQ should have a floor area large enough to lie down on. This will be useful for practising sit-ups and push-ups to improve your basic fitness — essential for the best spies.

- Your HQ must include a desk at which to plan missions. A desk offers plenty of hiding places for secret documents, as well as providing ample room to create anti-snooping devices and space for mastering code-breaking techniques (see pages 120-123).

Make sure you are seen sitting at your desk doing homework regularly, so no one questions what you are doing sitting at it.

- A mirror is a vital piece of equipment for many reasons. You will be able to use it when creating a disguise and to check your appearance before leaving HQ. It will also provide defence against surprise visits (see pages 14-15). The best kind of mirror to get is one on a stand, whose angle you can adjust depending on whether you are using it to put on disguises or keeping an eye on the door to your HQ.

- Hang a framed photograph or picture on the wall — a picture of you looking your best is always nice. On the front is an innocent-looking you — on the reverse attach a clear plastic document folder into which you can slip the outline of your latest mission, or coded messages that need to be broken. Simply flip the picture over according to who is in HQ at the time.

- Buy a flat map of your local area. This is invaluable for plotting the route of your missions. If your bedroom has a roller blind, pull it down and secure the map to the front of it — just pull the cord to make it disappear in a flash. Alternatively, stick your map to a sheet of cardboard that can be slipped behind your wardrobe when not in use.

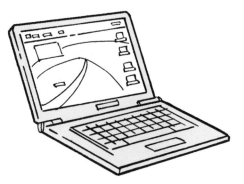

OTHER ESSENTIAL ITEMS

- a torch
- a small notebook
- some pens and pencils
- paper and card supplies
- paintbrushes
- sticky tack
- sticky tape
- chalk
- scissors
- small mirrors
- talcum powder
- junk, such as tin cans, toilet rolls, juice cartons, rope, bamboo canes
- unusual clothing for disguises, or a collection of coats, hats, scarves
- some dark glasses

USEFUL, BUT NON-ESSENTIAL ITEMS

- a computer
- a camera phone
- face paints
- tarpaulin sheet
- a pair of binoculars

HOW TO ...
SET UP AN ADVANCE WARNING SYSTEM

As a spy, security is one of your top priorities. To keep your secrets safe, it's vital to stay on the look-out for 'unfriendlies' (siblings, parents and rival agents). A few seconds' warning may be all you have to ensure you aren't taken unawares. Use any of these simple precautions to protect your HQ:

- Balance an empty tin can on the door handle inside the room. Anyone trying the door will dislodge the can, warning you of a potential intruder and giving you time to conceal your secret files.

- Angle a mirror so that you always have a view of the door to your room. This way no one can sneak up on you.

- Keep your HQ dimly lit and the light in the corridor outside your room on. This will help you to keep an eye out for shadows under the door, created by anyone standing behind it listening.

HOW TO ...
SET UP
A BALANCE ALARM

Vary the combinations each time you use this alarm.

A balance alarm will guarantee that
any snoops are caught out.

1   Number the toilet rolls, 1 to 3, so you can identify them.

2   Stand the rolls just behind the door to HQ as you leave.

3   Balance a pen or pencil on top of each roll. Note which coloured pen is on which of the numbered toilet rolls and the order of the numbers from left to right.

4   When you return to base, you will be able to tell if anyone has been inside, knocked over the balance alarm and tried to cover their tracks. It's very unlikely that the toilet rolls will be in the correct order right to left, with the correct pen or pencil on top.

POINT THE FINGER AT AN INTRUDER

The most dangerous time for your HQ is when you are away from it. If you think someone may try to infiltrate HQ, make use of these measures:

- Pull a hair from your head and cover it in spit. As you leave your HQ, close the door behind you and stick the damp hair across the gap between the door and the doorframe. If anyone goes in while you are out, the hair will drop off and you'll know you've had a 'visit'.

- If you have a camera phone, take a photo of your HQ each time you leave. When you get back, compare the picture with the scene in front of you. Try to spot differences that indicate someone has been rifling through your stuff.

- Maintain top-level security by keeping spy files in alphabetical order — except for one. A rival rooting through will probably put them all back in perfect alphabetical order — a major snoop alert.

If you think your HQ has been penetrated, here's a great way to track down the culprit:

1 Sprinkle talcum powder at the door to your HQ – a fine layer on the carpet or floor, that an intruder won't notice.

2 When you return, check the floor for footprints. If anyone has been in, they will have left tracks in the powder. Check the shoes in the cupboards of everyone in your household for talc on the soles. You will soon have the culprit.

POINTING THE FINGER

Whenever you touch an object with your bare hands, tiny amounts of sweat and oil from your skin are left behind as fingerprints. These are identical copies of the ridged patterns on your fingertips. No two people have the same fingerprints, which means you can compile a record of the prints left after any break-ins and hopefully use them to find out exactly who has entered your spy HQ.

Why not plan ahead and build up a library of the prints of people who are often in your bedroom? In an emergency, you can compare a suspect print against your print library and make a positive match more quickly.

The key to lifting a copy of a fingerprint from a surface is to use a fine powder that will stick to the greasy residue left behind. This will enable you to take a 'print'. Here's how to become a top print analyst:

YOU WILL NEED

• a paintbrush • some sticky tape
• a pencil • a sharpener • a nail file
• a sheet of white paper

1 Make your own fingerprint dust with a pencil and nail file by sharpening the pencil and then rubbing away at the graphite point with the file. This gives you a dark-coloured powder, or graphite dust, that will show up against the white paper.

2 Sprinkle the graphite dust lightly over the suspect fingerprint.

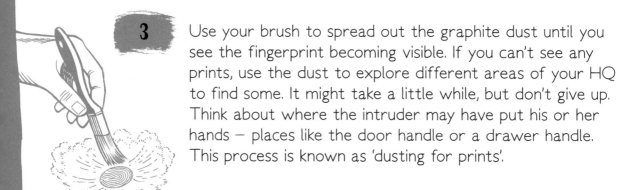

3 Use your brush to spread out the graphite dust until you see the fingerprint becoming visible. If you can't see any prints, use the dust to explore different areas of your HQ to find some. It might take a little while, but don't give up. Think about where the intruder may have put his or her hands — places like the door handle or a drawer handle. This process is known as 'dusting for prints'.

4 Once you've tracked down a fingerprint, you need to capture, catalogue and identify it. To do this, place a piece of tape, sticky-side down, over the print. Make sure that the tape is large enough to cover the whole print. Press firmly on the tape over the print, then peel it off again carefully. You should be able to see the print clearly on the tape.

5 Stick the tape containing the print on to a sheet of white paper and label it with details of where it was found and the date.

6 Track down the owner of the print and the identity of the intruder by checking it against the prints of your friends and members of your family. Get them to press each of their fingertips on to a clean, shiny surface and take their prints using the method just described.

If you're going to use this method, it's a good idea to clean the surface of your desk and the fronts of your drawers and cupboards with a damp, soapy cloth before you leave your HQ. This cleans the scene and ensures your fingerprints or historic prints do not confuse the situation.

HAVE THE BEST SECRET HIDING PLACES

Ideally, you would be able to flip a switch and make the walls of your HQ rotate so that all of your secret spy equipment instantly disappeared from sight. Unfortunately, this doesn't tend to happen in the real world. You'll need to find the perfect hiding places for your code books, spy lists and reports, to keep them safe from prying eyes, double agents or, worst of all, an adult!

Fold your secret papers up small enough to fit inside a stinky trainer, pop them inside and cover with a smelly sock to repel snoopers.

IN PLAIN SIGHT

If you ever have to hide a file in a hurry, it is essential to have worked out a good hiding place in advance. The more untidy your HQ is, the easier it will be to hide things 'in plain sight'. This means that a file can be right under a snooper's nose without them realizing it. However, if your parents have that weird thing about tidiness, here are some alternative suggestions for slipping things out of sight in a split second:

- Slide secret papers underneath a rug, between books on your book shelves, or under your mattress. Tape a clear plastic folder (the kind people put sheets of paper in to keep them safe) to the underside of a drawer. You can easily slip papers in and out of these handy hold-alls.

- When you're working on an important secret email or text document, open a second, innocent-looking 'decoy' window on your computer's desktop. Make sure the decoy window is large enough to conceal the whole desktop. If you're interrupted, 'hot-switch' to your decoy window by using 'alt' + 'tab' for a PC or '⌘' + 'tab' if you are using a Macintosh computer.

- Tape any sensitive material to the back of a framed picture — only the most professional enemy agent will ever think to look there.

These ideas are great for short-term solutions, but all good spies play the 'long game', which means preparing in advance to create a secure and permanent hiding place. It's a bit more effort, but it will pay off in the end — there are some great long-term solutions throughout this book.

HOW TO ...
SPOT A GOOD SPY

The most successful espionage agents are so good at what they do, that it's usually impossible to tell that they are spies at all. Whether you're an agent working solo or seeking new recruits, you need to know the qualities that make some people more suited to spycraft than others. Use the following questions to check your own potential spy skills or to distinguish high-quality individuals from the crowd.

IS YOUR SUBJECT FIT AND ACTIVE?

Top spies are certainly no couch potatoes. They need to be fit, active and ready for anything in case they are sent on dangerous missions. It is important to know whether your subjects can keep up.

- Can they swim?
- Can they cycle or skateboard?
- Can they tie knots?
- Can they ski?

The more of these skills a recruit can master, the better. If subjects don't score very highly in this area, suggest that they take up a sport, such as swimming or jogging, to build up their strength and stamina. Any race against time will be tough going for an unfit agent.

CAN YOUR SUBJECT KEEP A SECRET?

If you suspect your 'subject' (the person you are considering recruiting) is a bit of a blabber-mouth, ask a fellow agent to test the subject with fake information. The agent should tell them a 'secret' such as:

'My sister has an extra toe,'
or
'Michael has green wee'.

If, next time you see them, your subject can't resist telling you what they have heard, you'll know they find it hard to keep quiet, and may not be the best person to join your operation.

IS YOUR SUBJECT ABLE TO IMPROVISE?

One of the most exciting things about being a spy is the unpredictable nature of your life. You never know what operation you might have to mount, what might happen and where you might end up. This means that the ability to improvise (this means to think quickly and work with whatever is lying around) is vital.

IS YOUR SUBJECT OBSERVANT?

All good spies have to keep their eyes and ears open at all times. You never know when you might come across an important piece of information or take a suspect by surprise. Even the smallest detail can turn out to be the key to completing a mission successfully. Try out your subject's observational skills with the memory tests on pages 37-39. Anyone who doesn't make the grade, shouldn't make the cut.

Make an assessment sheet for your dossier and mark potential recruits out of ten in each of the categories listed below.

SKILLS ASSESSMENT SHEET

Use the points below to work out how well-suited your recruits are to becoming a trainee spy. Mark them out of ten for each point — a score of 30 or above means that they should make a useful addition to your spy ring.

- ☐ Has the ability to keep things to themself
- ☐ Shows good attention to detail
- ☐ Keeps in good physical and mental shape
- ☐ Can blend in with the crowd
- ☐ Thinks on their feet and copes with the unexpected

HOW TO ...
CREATE THE PERFECT COVER STORY

If people begin to get suspicious about all the comings and goings in your spy HQ, or see you rummaging around in the undergrowth in your local park and wonder why, you'll need to create a cover story to explain your strange behaviour. The right story will stop people worrying what you're up to and provide a reasonable excuse for what you are doing at the same time.

- Claim that you've formed a wildlife club. There's nothing you enjoy more than studying animal antics in the local park. This way you can carry out 'dead-letter drops' (see pages 44-47) again and again without drawing suspicion.

- Announce that you and your friends have started a book group – this gives everyone in your spy ring a great reason for being in spy HQ all the time. Just remind everyone to bring matching books along to each visit.

- Tell people that you and your friends are helping each other study. Make sure that agents bring some genuine homework when they visit your house as proof of this.

CODE-NAME COVER-UP

Give each agent a code name that is linked to your cover story to add credibility. For example, if you tell everyone that you are in a wildlife club, each agent's code name could be a particular animal or bird, such as: 'Hawk', 'Fox' or 'Snake'.

If your cover story is a book group, why not give each agent the name of a favourite writer? Your code names could include: 'Pullman', 'Rowling' and 'Dahl'. Or, if you decided to tell people that your spy ring is a study group, each agent's code name could refer to their 'specialist subject', such as maths ('Number-cruncher'), science ('Physics-whiz'), or English ('Word-wizard').

FANCY THAT!

If you are caught on a mission in full disguise by a close friend or member of your family who recognizes you, it is essential to always carry a fake invite to a fancy dress party. All you need to do is pull out the invite and announce you are on the way to the party to explain away your strange appearance.

BUILD A CAMOUFLAGED DEN

If you're lucky enough to have a large garden or have access to an outdoor space, why not build your own all-weather, camouflaged spying den?

YOU WILL NEED

- 3 bamboo canes, roughly 1.5 m long
- 1 bamboo cane, roughly 2 m long
- a ball of string • scissors • large, old plastic sheeting
- a groundsheet, or a large bed sheet
- some heavy stones • a trowel

1 Decide where you want to position your den. Look for a sheltered position, out of the wind, and preferably on slightly raised ground for drainage. A good solid tree with a forked branch can form the back of your shelter, but a bush or wall works just as well.

2 Create a frame for your shelter by taking the three shorter bamboo canes and lashing them together with a length of string, about 15 cm from the top, to form a tripod.

3 Place the final cane into the forks of the supporting canes to form a ridge pole. Tie it securely with string. Rest the ridge pole in the branch of a tree, then push the supporting poles into the ground at a 45° angle. Check that these supports are firmly rooted in the ground. Alternatively, rest the ridge pole securely in a bush or on top of a wall.

4 Lay the sheeting over the frame, leaving an opening at the front so that you can get in and out easily. There should be enough fabric to overlap at the front and keep out breezes. Place the stones along the two edges of your sheeting that touch the ground to weigh it down and stop it blowing away in the wind.

5 Clear the ground inside your shelter so that it is comfortable to sit on. Lay down the groundsheet or bed sheet.

6 Camouflage your den by plastering wet leaves, mud, light fallen branches or grass over the sheeting. This will also add an extra layer of insulation, making it warmer.

7 Use the trowel to dig a narrow trench around the sides and back of your den. This will channel rainwater away from the inside and help to keep you dry.

8 Furnish your den with cushions or camp chairs. Sit back and get ready for your first meeting.

HOW TO ...

CREATE A QUICK DISGUISE

Even as a trainee spy, you should already be paying attention to how you think and behave as a spy – starting with your outfits. Your spy kit should contain at least one item that can be used if you realize you are being tailed at any point on a mission. It should be something that will instantly change your appearance, and will not be out of place in any situation.

Never use sunglasses as a disguise indoors, or during the winter months — you are more likely to draw attention to yourself.

A HAT

Make sure that you select a good spy hat. This should be a hat you can tuck easily into your pocket, so you can put it on or take it off whenever you need to. A good spy hat should be easy to pull down over your hair and eyes. It should be versatile, which means it should be one that you can wear in a variety of ways — like a woollen hat that you can wear rolled up or rolled down.

SUNGLASSES

On a warm, sunny day, what could be more normal than wearing sunglasses? Slip on some shades to look instantly incognito. Not only will you disguise your identity, you'll also make it harder for other people to see exactly where you are looking, putting you at an advantage.

A SCARF

Keep a scarf in your bag to wrap around your neck at a moment's notice. A dark, plain scarf is better than brightly-coloured checks, for example. You don't want to stick out like a sore thumb.

LAYERS

Several thin layers of clothing, such as a couple of differently-coloured T-shirts, a thin sweater, a hooded top and a light coat, give you lots of options for changing your appearance on a mission. Put whatever layers you are not wearing in a rucksack, or change the order of the layers to give you a completely different appearance.

HOW TO ...
SHADOW
A SUSPECT

Shadowing is one of the most important skills that a spy can master. Shadowing means that you can follow a target to find out just what they are up to, without ever being noticed.

Use shop windows, car windows or mirrors, to keep an eye on your target's movements. Practise sharpening your peripheral vision, so that when you are looking straight ahead you can still watch your target out of the corners of your eyes.

SHADOWING SECRETS

SIMPLE DISGUISE. Hide your identity — dark glasses to cover your eyes or a hat to conceal your hair will be fine. You'll need to dress in dark, muted colours, which means leave your favourite red jumper at home.

SUPPLIES AT THE READY. Carrying money and travel passes at all times is essential in case your target boards a bus or train. You wouldn't want to get left behind at the bus stop.

TARGET IDENTITY. It may sound obvious, but make sure you're shadowing the right person — memorize their appearance on the day. It would be embarrassing to realize you had shadowed the wrong person for several hours.

KEEP YOUR DISTANCE. Don't act as if you actually are your target's shadow — if they trip right over you, your presence will definitely be revealed. There's no need to get too close to your target. Try to stay on the opposite side of the street or a decent distance behind.

STOP-START TECHNIQUE. If your target comes to a halt while walking, you should carry on walking. Then find an opportunity to stop a little further on. Try to vary your reason for stopping. You might be able to tie your laces once or twice without being noticed, but you will give the game away if you do it more often. Pause to look in shop windows, ask a passer-by for directions, or check your mobile phone for messages.

KEEP UP. If your target seems to be getting too far ahead, don't walk faster or start to run — this will attract attention and risk blowing your cover. Instead, increase the length of your stride until you have caught up a little. If your target 'vanishes' around a bend, simply sprint to reach the corner quickly. Just before you get to it, slow down to make sure you walk around the corner at your usual pace.

TEST YOUR TRAINING

Now you know how to follow a target, it's time to put your shadowing skills to the test by practising with a friend. Here's how:

1 Arrange to meet a friend somewhere busy — such as at the local shops. Use the shadowing secrets on pages 34 and 35 to follow your target all the way from their house to the meeting point without being spotted. Don't be too ambitious — following a friend on their family holiday could probably prove tricky.

2 Take a camera phone with you, if you have one, to detail their movements. Follow your target as they go about their business. At various stages, pretend to make a phone call, but take snaps or video footage of them instead. If you don't have a camera phone, use a small notebook and pen to jot down details of their movements.

3 Once your friend arrives at the pre-arranged location, innocently pretend to turn up for your meeting. Later, once your friend has returned home, pop round to show them the evidence of how well you tailed them throughout the day.

TEST A SPY'S MEMORY

Here is a test to help you keep a recruit's memory sharp.

WHAT'S MISSING?

Place a dozen small items on a tray and give your recruit a minute to memorize them. Take the tray out of the room, remove three items and move the remaining objects around. Return to the room and ask your spy to tell you which items have gone. Remove another three objects and ask your recruit which objects are missing again. Do this once more so there are just three items left on the tray.

Mark recruits' scores out of ten. Record the results using the chart template on page 127.

- Award one point for each item remembered.

- Give one bonus point if recruits remember all nine removed objects.

Don't give up if your potential recruit doesn't do well first time. The brain is a muscle which gets stronger with practice. Repeat the tasks and you should see an improvement in your recruits' scores. You'll soon have a crack team of super-agents.

SCENE IT

Root through your photo albums, old postcards, or newspapers and magazines to find some pictures of busy street scenes. Give your recruit one minute to study the scene. Now ask them five questions about the scene. For example:

- 'How many people are wearing hats?'

- 'What colour was the car in the picture?'

- 'Was the person riding a bicycle male or female?'

You are testing their powers of recall and their ability to remember details. Mark recruits' scores out of ten and record the results using the chart template on page 127.

- Give one point for each correct answer.

- Award a bonus point for extra detail on each question.

IT'S ALL IN THE DETAIL

This final task will demonstrate a recruit's ability to remember details about people's appearances.

Show your recruit a photograph of a person randomly selected from a magazine. Allow them one minute to study it, then hide the picture. Get your recruit to give you five clear, accurate details about the person in the picture. So, rather than, 'He is medium height, medium brown hair, blue coat,' look for interesting descriptions, such as, 'He looked about 17, with short dark curly hair, and a mole on his right cheek.' This is just the kind of information that really helps to track the right people down and helps to avoid a mistaken identity.

Record recruits' scores out of ten using the chart template on page 127.

- Give one point for each correct description.

- Award a bonus point for extra detail on each description.

HOW TO ...
HAVE FUN
WITH PHONETICS

In the phonetic alphabet each letter is assigned a specific word, so that it is impossible to mistake one letter for another in a radio or telephone conversation. You can use it to make sure your messages aren't misunderstood. Here's how:

Whenever you need to make sure a word or name is clear, simply use the list below to spell it out. You could even give yourselves your own 'call signs' — perfect when you want to be clear which person is speaking over a walkie-talkie.

Replace each of your initials with the phonetic alphabet words that represent them. So, if your name happened to be Louise Martin, your call sign would be 'Lima Mike'.

PHONETIC ALPHABET

A	Alfa	J	Juliet	S	Sierra
B	Bravo	K	Kilo	T	Tango
C	Charlie	L	Lima	U	Uniform
D	Delta	M	Mike	V	Victor
E	Echo	N	November	W	Whiskey
F	Foxtrot	O	Oscar	X	X-Ray
G	Golf	P	Papa	Y	Yankee
H	Hotel	Q	Quebec	Z	Zulu
I	India	R	Romeo		

PLAN AN UNDERCOVER MISSION

Good planning is vital to the success of any mission, whether you're staging a rescue, on the look-out for enemy agents, or just staking out the local park. Here's how to make sure that every spy mission goes off without a hitch.

Make sure you go through the plan with everyone thoroughly.

1   Create a 'mission dossier' — a safe place to store and access all the information you need for each mission. This could be a folder on a computer, or simply a paper document, but make sure it is well hidden and protected (see pages 22-23 and 80-81).

2   Make sure that all agents know exactly what the mission goal is and what you intend to do. Keep the details simple and clear. It should be something like 'find enemy code wheel' (see pages 76-79 for how to make one).

3   Assign a clear task to each agent, so everyone knows exactly what is expected of them. In addition, each agent should know the tasks of all the other agents.

4   First perform a 'recce' (short for 'reconnaissance' mission). This means that you scout out the location of the mission in advance. Wear a disguise so that you aren't noticed, and take a camera if possible. Note down any obstacles, guards or weak spots that might make your mission easier.

5   Prepare a back-up plan and rendezvous point in case anything goes wrong.

6   Write everything listed opposite in your mission dossier — include photos and any relevant information from your recce. Then gather your fellow spies and discuss it all.

7   If there is time, have a practice run of the mission in advance. Check that the plan works well and that everyone knows what they are doing. If there is no time for this, make sure you go through the plan with everyone thoroughly.

8   After the mission, gather your agents together and hold a 'debriefing' (where everyone describes exactly what happened to them on the mission). Discuss what went right and what went wrong, so you learn from your experiences.

HOW TO ...
SET UP A DEAD-LETTER DROP

A dead-letter drop offers a safe and discreet way for fellow spies to communicate without the risk of actually meeting in person. It should be located in a place where the message can be left for pick-up by a fellow spy at a later time.

SECRETS OF SUCCESS

When choosing a dead-letter drop, always bear in mind that the hiding place should be:

INCONSPICUOUS. A park, street or café where lots of people are milling around are better places for dead-letter drops than an isolated area where you would be easily spotted.

WELL-HIDDEN. You don't want innocent (or not-so-innocent) people to stumble across your message. Think about animals, too — a nosy bird or squirrel might eat or move your message if it is in an obvious spot.

ROUTINE ROUTES

Think of a place near a path you often take — perhaps on the way to the high street, school or park. People may get suspicious if you have to think up a reason for going somewhere new each time you want to make a drop.

If you have a dog, taking it for a walk makes a great cover. Next time you're out with Rover, subtly scout around for a distinctive rock (large enough to conceal a message) or a hollow in a tree.

COVERT SUGGESTIONS

Stuck for ideas of where to make your first drop? Here are some pointers:

Don't forget to protect your message from the elements. Wrap it up in a plastic bag, so that it's water-tight. Make sure it is stuck down securely. It may be a while before your contact can pick it up and you don't want it to come loose, which could lead to it being discovered.

Park benches are great places for dead-letter drops. What could be more natural than having a sit down? While you're doing that, could you stick your message under the bars of the seat?

CHECK YOUR BEARINGS

If there is a street sign at the end of your road, check to see how much room is behind it. Could you quickly tape a message there without prying eyes noticing? No one will look there, except for your contact.

AT THE MOVIES

Plan well in advance to agree the name and number of the seat you will use, then stick your message just under the right-hand arm while you are watching the film. The darkness offers perfect cover for the drop and your contact can pick up the message at the next screening.

SAFE AND DISCREET

Check the location works well for your contact, too. Then, when you need to leave your message, stop to tie your shoelace or pat your dog next to the rock or tree. While you're doing that, drop off your secret message.

Make a couple of test runs first, but leave meaningless messages. Double back to check if they have been discovered or if your contact has picked them up.

HOW TO ...
DISGUISE YOUR MESSAGES

As soon as you write down secret information on paper your spy ring is vulnerable to infiltration (allowing sneaks and snoops to gain access to your group). This is why a wise spy goes to great lengths to disguise the secrets they are passing on by using codes and ciphers. Use these cryptic techniques to keep your secrets safe.

CODE ONE: SUBSTITUTION

The simplest way to encode your communications is to substitute each letter in your message for another. Here's how:

1 Write out the alphabet. Then write it out again underneath, but starting one place to the right — A below B, B below C, and so on, round to Z below A. This is your key.

A	B	C	D	E	F	G	H	I	J	K	L	M
Z	A	B	C	D	E	F	G	H	I	J	K	L

N	O	P	Q	R	S	T	U	V	W	X	Y	Z
M	N	O	P	Q	R	S	T	U	V	W	X	Y

2 Substitute the letter you want for the letter underneath and write out your coded message. So, 'Come to HQ after school' becomes, 'Bnld sn GP zesdq rbgnnk.'

3 Change your key regularly, varying the letter at which you start the substitute alphabet — it could be three or twenty places along. To show the decoder which letter you have substituted for A, make a tiny pin prick under that letter the first time it is used. For example, if you have substituted Z for A, as described above, make the pinprick under the first Z in the message.

4 When you have finished writing the coded message, destroy your key to stop it falling into enemy hands.

Write your message out with the spaces added randomly, so that they do not correspond to the real breaks in words. This will make the message even harder to work out.

CODE TWO: PIGPEN

This code is almost impossible to decipher unless you know the secret.

1   Draw two separate grids and write the alphabet in the grids, with two letters in each box of the grid — as shown opposite.

2   To write out the pigpen alphabet the first letter in each box is shown with only the lines that surround it, the second is shown with the lines and a dot. 'A' is shown as ⌐, 'B' is ⌐ and so on.

So, 'Meet at three in the park', would look like this:

⌐LL ∨ ∨ ∴⌐LL □⌐∨ ∷L⌐ ⌐

3   You can now assign a symbol to each letter, using the section of its grid as a guide. Remember to add a dot to indicate that the letter is the second one within each box.

4   Make sure that all your agents know how you are writing out the alphabet and which grid you have put the letters into.

CODE THREE: SWAP-SHOP

This code is based on swapping and reswapping the letters in a message.

1 First, write out a message, such as:

> 'Meet at three in the park.'

2 Now write the words in reverse order:

> 'park the in three at meet.'

3 Then swap the first and last letter of each word:

> 'karp eht ni ehret ta teem.'

4 Add two random letters, such as 'ed' or 'er' at the beginning or end of every other word to finish your cipher:

> 'Karped eht nied ehret taed teem.'

Make sure that each member of your spy ring understands how to decipher this type of message.

CODE FOUR: MAD-MEN

If you're ever pressed for time and have to whisper a message rather than write it down, it is still possible to encode it. Try this spoken code for a quick solution.

Add the word 'mad' in front of spoken vowels in each word. So a message such as, 'Help! Base is surrounded', becomes:

> 'Hmadelp! Bmadase madis smadurrmadomadundmaded'.

HOW TO ...

USE HAND SIGNALS WHILE ON OPERATION

Your mission has been a success. Your agents are within earshot of the enemy. It's vital that you give them instructions, but how? A walkie-talkie, even a whisper, could give away your positions. Here's your guide to some of the basic hand signals you need to know to communicate with your agents.

One

Two

Three

Four

Five

Six

Seven

Eight

52

Nine

Ten

You

Me

Come this way

Stop

Move faster

Walk in pairs

Single file

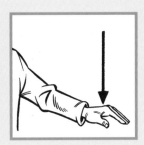

Get down

Understood/Okay

Not understood

Rendezvous

Don't forget to practise so that your entire team knows what each gesture means and won't misunderstand an instruction.

HOW TO ...
BE THE BEST AT READING BODY LANGUAGE

Reading codes is one thing but reading people's inner thoughts is altogether trickier. Does a smile mask an unpleasant intent? Should you trust that conversation, or is the messenger leading you into a trap? Is that really an innocent passer-by?

If you can decode body language, you'll be able to reveal someone's true feelings. So whenever you're talking to a contact or another spy, focus on their faces and what they're doing. You may be surprised by what they're really thinking.

WARNING SIGNS

Look out for any of the following clues from people you talk to — they should send your spy antennae into overdrive:

- Do they raise their lip and wrinkle their nose? This means they find something you've said or something about you unpleasant.

- Do they smile for longer than a second, without the muscles around their eyes moving? This is a sure sign that the smile is fake.

- Are they picking at their clothes and/or looking at the floor? This can mean that they don't approve of your orders but aren't saying so. Defuse the situation by reassuring them and allowing them to discuss their concerns openly.

- Do they keep moving from one foot to the other? If they can't stand still or look at you, it's a sign that they are feeling guilty about something. Either that or they need to go to the toilet!

- Do they keep rubbing at the back of their head? This can suggest impatience. Watch out for an emotional outburst — or try to calm them down and let them speak their mind first.

- Are they standing with their arms crossed? This is a sure sign that they are angry and spoiling for a fight. Remain calm and alert, but don't let them out of your sight!

- Do they keep checking their hands, or looking at the time? This means that they are seriously bored. You'll need to make things a little more interesting if you're going to keep your spy ring going.

- If they narrow their eyes and tilt their head back, this is a real danger sign that someone doesn't like you. Watch out!

TELL A LIE FROM THE TRUTH

Most people find it impossible to control the things they do involuntarily when they tell a lie. There are lots of tell-tale signs that can give away a double-crossing double agent. For example, you may notice their nose becomes redder, or that their pupils dilate, becoming much larger than usual. Here are some other things that may signal they're not telling the truth:

- touching their nose a lot

- refusing to make eye contact

- sweating a lot

- biting their nails

- talking too much, with too much detail

- making dramatic hand gestures.

If you're in the company of someone who sympathizes with you or believes in you, they will start to unconsciously mirror the gestures you make. To test this, slowly cross one leg over the other and wait. The person you're with should mimic that move if they admire you. Keep your movements natural and try another gesture, such as leaning forwards. Again, they should copy you.

MAKE A SNOOPER PAPER

A newspaper is not only useful for keeping up with what's going on in the world around you. A spy would use one to shield his face from passing gazes and to blend into the background. This is even more effective with your own 'Snooper Paper'. Here's how to make one:

YOU WILL NEED

- a newspaper
- a sharp pencil
- a blob of sticky tack

1. Remove the cover of your newspaper (you'll need this later). Open the remaining paper at the middle pages and place it with the middle pages face down on a table.

2. Place the blob of sticky tack under the first few pages of the paper, roughly 5 cm from the top and 5 cm from the centre. Use the point of the pencil to pierce an eyehole through to the sticky tack, as shown.

3. Work through the rest of the newspaper in the same way, a few sheets at a time, creating an eyehole. Make sure the eyehole lines up through each layer.

4. Repeat on the opposite side to make the other eyehole – making sure the holes are the correct distance apart for you to see through.

5. On the newspaper cover, make two new eyeholes, 5 cm either side of the centre, but this time, 7 cm from the top.

6. Test your Snooper Paper by lining up the layers. Slip the cover upwards by 2 cm to line up the final layer. You'll be able to see through the eyeholes, but as soon as you lower the cover, the holes will disappear.

You're ready to take up position on a stake out and use your Snooper Paper to track targets without being noticed. If you suspect that anyone has rumbled you, slip the cover down to block the eyeholes, roll up the paper and walk away as casually as possible.

BECOME A REAL-LIFE SPY

To be a real spy, you'll need the eyesight of an eagle, the reflexes of an Olympic athlete, and the skills of a martial arts expert. Right? Not necessarily. Opportunities to become a spy can be open to ordinary people, too.

CRACK COMMUNICATOR

People who can translate conversations or documents from other languages are always needed. Do you speak another language?

TOP-TECH

If you're good with computers, you could find yourself tracking and tracing information, testing system security and bugging important conversations.

LIFE-LONG LEADER

If you're a natural leader, you could find the perfect role running your own real-life spy ring, briefing agents.

ORGANIZED INTELLIGENCE

With so many agents in the field, spy rings need highly-organized people to sort through all the information they receive.
How organized are you?

HOW TO ...

PURSUE A SUSPECT

ON TOP OF A MOVING TRAIN

WARNING

Never give this a try in the real world — not only would you be arrested, but it would be incredibly dangerous as well. Leave these antics in the safe hands of James Bond's stunt co-ordinator.

Don't rush! Your suspect will not be moving any faster!

Imagine you are tailing a suspect and they hot-foot it to Tibet on the Qingzang Railway – you'll obviously have to follow. When you're stuck on a train heading to Tibet it will be much more difficult to keep a low profile. If they get wise to you and try to make a getaway, you'll need to think fast to keep up, but would it ever really be possible to follow in the footsteps of James Bond and go after someone up top?

NECESSARY KNOW-HOW

Calling the guard or pulling the emergency cord might solve this problem without blowing your cover, but if you do find yourself on top of a moving train, here's how to follow:

1 Once you're up on the roof, kneel down and take a moment to get used to the motion of the train.

2 Don't try to stand up. Unless the train is moving at under 30 km an hour the wind resistance would knock you over anyway.

3 Look in the direction the train is travelling before you set off. Check for overhead hazards such as power cables and bridges, or trees and bushes.

4 Assuming the coast is clear, crawl along on all fours, or wriggle like a snake until you feel more confident.

5 If the train goes around a bend, lie flat and hang on to anything sticking up on the roof or 'grab rails' on the side.

6 Crouch down, then move with the rhythm of the train carriages. This will mean moving in a zigzag pattern. Adopt a crab-like or spider-like gait, keeping your feet apart for balance.

BECOME A SURVEILLANCE EXPERT

When you're on a surveillance mission, vigilance is key. Have you ever thought that sometimes it would be useful to have eyes in the back of your head? A pocket 'Sneakobook' is an easy way to give yourself exactly that advantage.
Here's how to make one:

YOU WILL NEED

- 2 small rectangular mirrors
- sticky tape • PVA glue
- an old hardback book you don't mind gluing

1 Place the two mirrors face down on a flat surface. Line up the long edges, so that there is a narrow gap between them, roughly 0.5 cm wide.

2 Get out the sticky tape and place a strip down the join. Add two or three extra strips for additional strength.

3 Turn over the mirrors, they should now be 'hinged' by the tape. Check that they bend back and forth easily.

4 Open your book to the middle pages and place the mirrors in the middle of them. Make sure that the mirrors don't stick out beyond the edges of the pages.

5 When the mirrors are in a good position — the book should open and close easily — cover the back of the mirrors with glue, then shut the book, so they are glued into place.

6 Once the mirrors are firmly in place, open the book and pretend to read. You should be able to angle the book so that you can easily look in the mirrors and see behind you.

On sunny days you need to be extremely careful to make sure the mirrors don't catch the sunlight and alert your 'mark' (the subject under surveillance) to your presence.

MAKE A CODE GRID

Code grids are an ingenious way to hide a secret message or communication within an apparently innocent document.

YOU WILL NEED

- 2 pieces of A4 card (or thick paper) • A4 sheet of graph paper • A4 sheet of blank paper • a pencil • a pair of scissors • some paper clips • a pin

1 Write down your secret message, and count how many letters it contains. Let's say your message is 'Meet me in ten minutes' – it contains 18 letters.

2 Use paper clips to fix the sheet of graph paper over the two pieces of card, then shade in 18 squares (one square for each letter in your message) in random places on the graph paper. Use a pin to mark the corners of the 18 squares. Push hard enough for the pinpricks to penetrate both the layers of card.

3 Using the pinpricks to guide you, cut these squares out of both pieces of card.

4   Unclip the cards and dispose of the graph paper.

5   Look closely at the pieces of card to make sure the holes are in identical positions. These are now your code grids. Pass one to your fellow agent and keep the other yourself.

6   Put one code grid over a blank sheet of paper and clip in place. Write your message in the holes — one letter per hole. Work left to right, going down the page as normal.

7   Fill the rest of the paper with other letters at random. You can even write whole sentences to make it appear just like any other innocent piece of paper.

8 Pass the message to your fellow agent.

9 The agent decoding the message just needs to place the code grid over the piece of paper, revealing only the letters that make up your message in the pattern of the grid.

Change grids regularly and build up a supply of them to use over time. That way, if one goes missing, or falls into the wrong hands, you will still be able to communicate with your fellow spies safely.

HOW TO ...
USE EMERGENCY SIGNALS

Codes are always an excellent way to communicate complicated messages, but sometimes something simpler and quicker will do. Here are a set of emergency signals your agents need to know about.

WINDOW SIGNALS

Place certain objects on the windowsill of your bedroom window (also known as spy HQ) to send clear messages to fellow spies.

- An empty drinks bottle says 'the coast is clear, come on in'.

- A rucksack alerts everyone the spy HQ should be avoided.

- A photo frame signals that everyone should meet at the usual place.

- The blind or curtain half drawn says 'call off the plan'.

PEN SIGNALS

Using a number of differently coloured pens, you can assign a code to each one to alert your fellow spies.

- Use a traffic light system – so that red means danger, green means all clear and yellow means be alert. Pop the pens into your blazer or shirt pocket, with the coloured lids showing.

- Agree a simple set of signals with your fellow spies. For instance, the pen on the left could be most important – the rest decoys. Your fellow spies will then be able to read the signal the pens make.

FACE SIGNALS

- Scratch your nose to signal 'danger, keep away'.

- Brush your eyebrow to say 'let's rendezvous at base'.

- Rub your right ear lobe to signal 'follow me'.

- Scratch your head to tell a fellow spy to follow the other person instead.

SIGNAL FROM A DISTANCE

Semaphore is a globally-recognized way of signalling information. To be a semaphore signaller, all you need are two 'flags' made from two differently coloured triangles. Don't worry if you can't find any proper semaphore flags — you can easily create your own. Here's how:

YOU WILL NEED

• 2 squares of brightly-coloured fabric, 30 cm by 30 cm • scissors • a needle and thread • 2 short bamboo canes

1. Ask your folks for some old shirts, tops or rags. Any fabric will do, so long as it's in bright, plain, contrasting colours. You'll need enough for two squares.

2. Cut each square of fabric into two triangles. You should have four triangles in total — two of each colour.

3. Sew the two contrasting triangles together along the diagonal line to create two flags, using a simple backstitch.

4. Root around in your garden for some bamboo canes.

5. Attach the bamboo canes to one edge of the fabric by rolling this edge of your flag around the pole and stitching along it. Make it a snug fit — you don't want your flag to slip when you are signalling. Sew up the top of the fabric so that the flag can't slip out of place.

6. Get plenty of practice extending your arms and holding the flags — semaphore can be a tiring business!

GETTING YOUR MESSAGE ACROSS

Once your flags are ready, you and your fellow spies need to learn the semaphore alphabet. There are several different positions for each arm: straight up, 45° down from vertical, straight out to the side, 45° down from horizontal, and straight down. To form some letters, you will need to hold one arm across your body as well. The position of each arm can be combined to form a code that corresponds to numbers and the letters of the alphabet.

SEMAPHORE SIGNALS

Here are the traditional semaphore signals for you to practise.
If you need to get someone's attention with your flags, simply flap
your arms up and down. If you make any mistakes, repeat the signal
for the letter 'E' (as in 'error') five times.

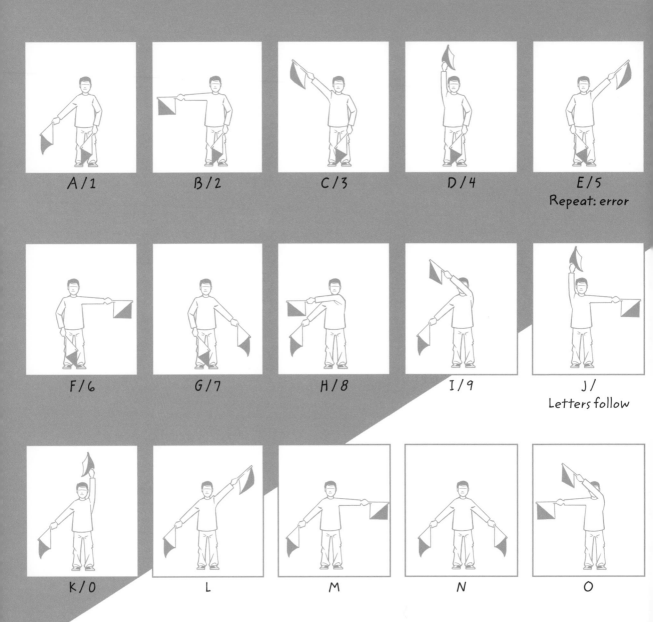

A/1   B/2   C/3   D/4   E/5
Repeat: error

F/6   G/7   H/8   I/9   J/
Letters follow

K/0   L   M   N   O

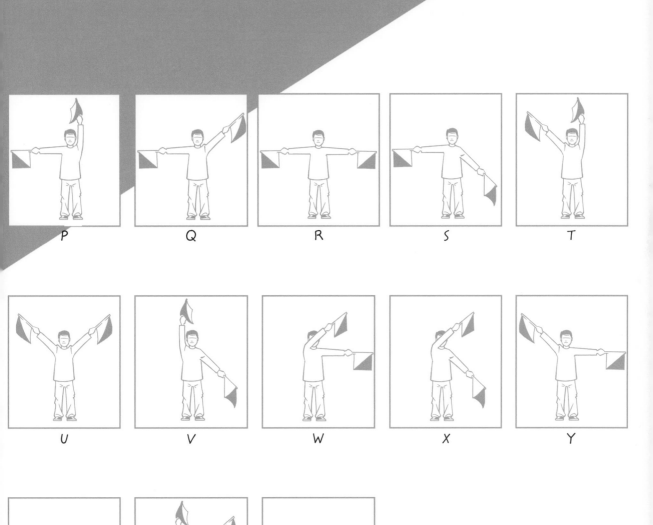

P   Q   R   S   T

U   V   W   X   Y

Z   Numbers follow   Pause

GOOD LUCK.

MAKE A
CODE WHEEL

A code wheel is easy to make, but creates a code that's almost uncrackable. You'll need to make two code wheels so that your message can be decoded by a fellow agent.

YOU WILL NEED

- a butterfly paper fastener
- a sheet of thick A4 paper
- a pair of compasses • scissors
- a ruler • a pencil and pen
- a protractor

1

Draw two circles on to your paper, 10.5 cm in diameter, using your compasses and a pencil and cut them both out. Draw two inner rings onto one, from the same centre point. One measuring 8.5 cm in diameter, the other measuring 6.5 cm in diameter.

2

Use your protractor to mark off 30 points around the edge of the smallest ring (each one will need to be at an angle of 12° from the next). Line your ruler up with the centre of the circle and one of the points you have marked on the inner ring. Draw a line with your pen from this point to the edge of the circle. Repeat with each point around the edge, as shown on the template on page 79.

3

Write the letters of the alphabet, plus a full stop, an apostrophe, a question mark and an exclamation mark, around the outer ring, in a clockwise direction. Use the inner ring to write the alphabet and punctuation marks out again, this time in an anti-clockwise direction, as shown on page 79.

To be even sneakier, you could write out both alphabet circles randomly for an utterly-uncrackable code.

4

Lay the second circle exactly over the other circle. Mark two windows on it, as shown in the diagram on page 79. One should line up over a letter in the outer alphabet ring and the other should line up over a letter in the inner ring. Carefully cut the two windows out.

5

To join the two circles together, line up the centres, with the alphabet circle at the bottom (there should still be marks from where you originally drew the circles). Make a hole with your pencil, then push the butterfly paper fastener through and split the ends to secure the two circles. The circles should both be able to rotate independently of each other.

6

Repeat steps 1 to 5 to make an exact duplicate code wheel. Hand this over to a fellow spy so they can decode your messages and send you their own.

USING THE WHEEL

To use your coding device, revolve the top wheel until it reveals the letter you need. Then look down to the notch on the opposite side and write down the letter displayed there. Continue until you have completely encoded your message.

The positioning of the two alphabet rings determines your code. Start the inner alphabet ring where 'T' appears on the outer ring, as shown, or pick another letter to make sure your code is different.

Shrewd spies can copy or trace over these templates and stick them onto circular pieces of card to add extra strength.

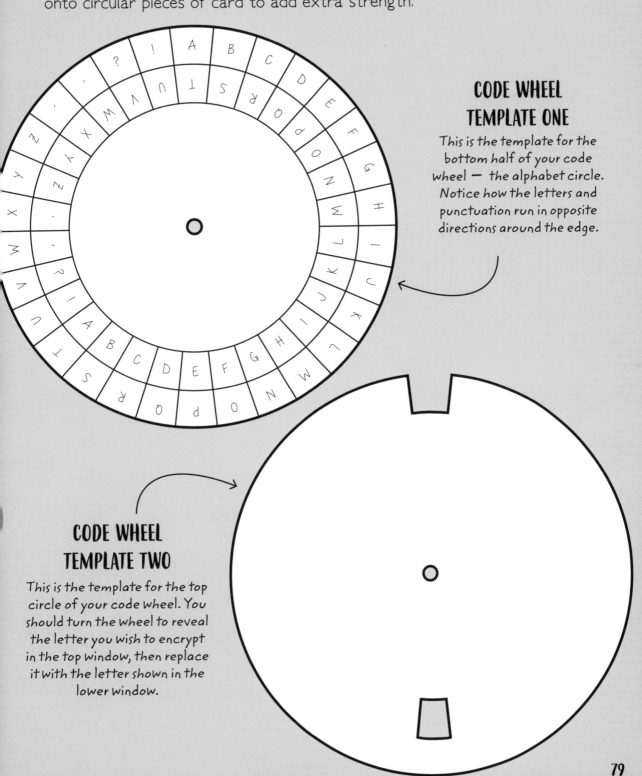

CODE WHEEL TEMPLATE ONE

This is the template for the bottom half of your code wheel — the alphabet circle. Notice how the letters and punctuation run in opposite directions around the edge.

CODE WHEEL TEMPLATE TWO

This is the template for the top circle of your code wheel. You should turn the wheel to reveal the letter you wish to encrypt in the top window, then replace it with the letter shown in the lower window.

HOW TO ...

CHOOSE A GOOD PASSWORD

Disguising and burying top-secret information on your computer should be enough to put most double agents off your trail, but there is an even better way to protect these documents: a well-chosen password.

ACCESS DENIED !!!!!

The way that you set up password protection will be different depending on the programme you use. As a guide, look for a 'Security' or 'Protection' heading, usually found within 'Tools', and follow the instructions there. If you can't find the right section, use the 'Help' facility available with your software.

Once you've found out how to set a password for a file, you'll need to choose a good one. Here are a few things you should (and shouldn't) do when setting a password:

DO

- Use a password that mixes numbers and letters, capitals and lower case letters.
- Choose a password that is at least six characters long.
- Avoid any word that you would find in a dictionary.
- Think of a memorable sentence. For instance: 'My best friend is called Jack Hardy'. Take the first letter of each word: m, b, f, i, c, j, h. Add in a capital letter and a digit to replace a letter, such as the number one for the letter 'i', for extra security and you have: 'mBf1cjh'.
- Choose two short words that wouldn't usually go together, such as 'bin' and 'roof'. Now add in some special characters again and you should come up with something like 'b1Nr00f'.
- Make sure that you don't use these examples!

DON'T

- Don't choose the word 'password'.
- Don't use any personal details — avoid your date of birth, your name, your pet's name or the name of anyone else in the family.
- Don't write your password down anywhere.
- Don't give your password to anyone else.
- Don't keep using the same password — change it at regular intervals.

MAKE YOUR ESCAPE

Even the most successful spies, such as Alex Ryder and James Bond, can find themselves overwhelmed by enemy agents. Imagine you were captured by a rival organization and held against your will. How would you escape?

ESCAPE FROM A PAIR OF HANDCUFFS

Handcuffs are impossible to open, right? Well, if you don't have any equipment, they are almost unbreakable. With the right tool, however, you can release them quite quickly. All you need is a simple, old-fashioned hairgrip. It is easy to hide one in the lining of a jacket or in a pocket, so make sure you have one within reach when you are captured. Try concealing it between your fingers or drop it on the floor within reach while you are being handcuffed. Then:

1 Once your captor has left the room, break the hairgrip so you can use the bendy section for grip and use the curved end for picking the lock.

2 Place the curved end into the keyhole on the cuffs, with the curve facing upwards. Make sure it's in the flat part of the keyhole, parallel with the handcuffs.

3 Apply steady pressure and push the grip forwards. The cuffs should spring open so that you can twist your hands out of them in one easy move.

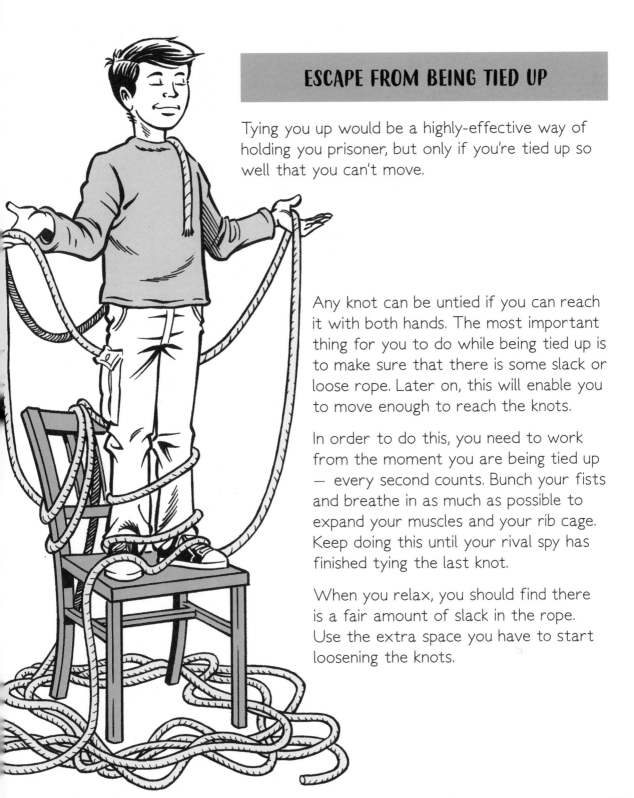

ESCAPE FROM BEING TIED UP

Tying you up would be a highly-effective way of holding you prisoner, but only if you're tied up so well that you can't move.

Any knot can be untied if you can reach it with both hands. The most important thing for you to do while being tied up is to make sure that there is some slack or loose rope. Later on, this will enable you to move enough to reach the knots.

In order to do this, you need to work from the moment you are being tied up — every second counts. Bunch your fists and breathe in as much as possible to expand your muscles and your rib cage. Keep doing this until your rival spy has finished tying the last knot.

When you relax, you should find there is a fair amount of slack in the rope. Use the extra space you have to start loosening the knots.

ESCAPE FROM A LOCKED ROOM

Now you're free from any handcuffs or ropes, but how do you get past a locked door?

1   First, check to see if the key has been left in the lock. If it has, hunt around the room that you have been locked in for any useful equipment. Ideally, you'll be able to find a large sheet of paper and a pen or pencil.

2   Lie on the floor so that you can see though the gap between the door and the floor. Make sure that no one is around outside to see what you are up to.

3   Carefully and quietly, slide the piece of paper under the gap in the door, so that the largest portion of it is directly below the lock on the opposite side of the door.

4   Use the pen or pencil, or the hairgrip if you still have it, to gently push the key out of the lock from your side of the door. As long as you don't push it too hard, the key should land on the piece of paper.

5   Pull the piece of paper slowly back towards you under the door, grab the key and make your escape.

WARNING

While it is fun to practise escape techniques with your friends, you never know when rival agents might swoop in and catch you off guard, so it is important to be sensible at all times. A true agent never plays practical jokes, such as leaving other agents tied up or locked in.

Keep an eye out for shadows
approaching as you work.

HOW TO ...
WRITE IN INVISIBLE INK

Mastering the art of writing invisible messages is vital for any spy. It makes it easy to pass secret communications between each other, because if they fall into the wrong hands you don't need to panic. Double agents, traitors or even parents won't realize what is going on. What's more, invisible writing is easy to achieve. Here's how:

YOU WILL NEED

- a juicy lemon • a calligraphy pen, or thin paintbrush
- some paper • a heat source (such as a light bulb,
a hairdryer, an iron or an oven)

1 Squeeze the juice out of the lemon and pick out the pips.

2 Dip your writing implement into the juice and write your message, plan or map onto the piece of paper. Write quickly, so that you can still see what you are writing before the juice dries.

3 Wait for the 'ink' to dry. As it does, your message should disappear.

4 Carrying or passing a blank piece of paper will raise suspicion, so you'll need to disguise the message. You can do this easily by flipping over the piece of paper and writing a 'normal' message on it. In addition, it's a good idea to sniff the message. If there's a tell-tale scent of lemon juice, borrow some perfume or aftershave and give the paper a quick squirt to mask the smell.

5 To reveal writing written with lemon juice, all you need to do is heat the paper up. There are lots of ways you can do this — try using a hairdryer to blow hot air onto it or hold it close to a light bulb. If neither of these methods work, ask an adult to pop the paper on a tray in a hot oven or run a warm iron over the back of the piece of paper.

6 Destroy the message after reading it.

Warning: Always be careful not to set your message on fire by overheating it.

TOP TIP

Try apple juice instead of lemon juice. Use a toothpick to collect juice from the apple and use it to write your message. Don't forget to eat the apple afterwards to destroy the evidence. You could even use milk to write with if all else fails.

ENCODE EMAILS QUICKLY

If you haven't got time for a complex encryption, use this super-speedy method to send an ultra-urgent email.

1   Type out your email as quickly as you can - make sure that no one is looking over your shoulder as you write.

2   Before you send it, highlight all of the text and change the font from letters into symbols. Anyone who spots it will just see nonsense, but the recipient can simply switch the writing back to letters to check your message, before quickly deleting it.

HOW TO ...
SHAKE OFF A TAIL

In the shadowy world of international espionage, a successful
spy is always alert and aware of the danger of being followed.
A 'tail' is a person who is secretly trying to follow you.
Practise the following evasion techniques in your local
area with fellow trainee agents, so you'll always have the
skills up your sleeve.

IN THE CITY

If your neck prickles and you get the feeling of being followed, it's vital to identify your tail quickly. To take a look behind you without arousing suspicion, try one of these two tricks:

- Find a shop selling something you might be genuinely interested in (rather than a wallpaper shop, for example).

- Stop, pretend to look at the window display, but then use the reflection in the glass to scan the street behind you.

- Stop at a parked car and pretend to be checking your hair in the window or wing mirror. While you're checking out your look, check out the people around you, too.

GIVE THEM THE SLIP

It's easier to shake off a tail if plenty of other people are around to give you cover — so head for a busy area.

- Look for a crowd of people to mingle among — as soon as you reach a side street or shop, slip out of sight.

- Stand casually by a bus stop. Once the bus pulls up, wait until the last possible moment to jump aboard. Time it just right and you should be able to leave your tail far behind.

- Casually and carefully cross to the opposite side of the street. When traffic blocks your shadow's eye-line, duck down a side street and watch to see if your ruse has worked.

IN THE COUNTRY

It's harder to shake off a tail if you're in the country or a quiet area. There are fewer distractions to help you disappear, but it also means that your tail will have to keep their distance to avoid being spotted. Use this factor to your advantage and gain a head start.

- Dead twigs and leaves can be a giveaway as you rustle through them. If you must walk across dry forest terrain, check where you step to avoid making too much noise. Walking backwards, sweeping leaves after each step to cover your tracks, may help to confuse your tail.

- Use muddy or sandy terrain to your advantage by setting a false trail. Leave clear tracks until you reach solid ground, then walk backwards in your original footprints before taking a different direction, covering your steps behind you.

- If you come across a shallow stream, this is an ideal opportunity to lose your tail. Simply walk in the stream bed for several metres before continuing on your way – your tail should not be able to see where the trail continues and will fall behind. Although you will end up with wet feet, it will be worth it in the end.

WARNING

Always make sure that a stream is shallow and
slow running so that it is safe enough to walk in.
You don't want it to turn into a torrent and sweep
you off your feet.

BE A MASTER OF DISGUISE

If you're trying to tail somebody who knows what you look like, you'll need to work much harder than usual to conceal your true identity. Try a combination of these top disguise tips to create a whole new you, or see pages 32 and 33 for some quick-fix disguises for when you're in a hurry.

- To make you look older and conceal your features, add some subtle facial hair. Keep it simple though — prepare a pair of sideburns from cotton wool glued onto pieces of card rather than trying to make a whole fake beard.

- Make yourself look larger by wearing lots of additional layers. Tie a cushion around your waist and add a thick coat or large jumper to cover it.

- Add instant grey by dusting your hair and eyebrows with talcum powder.

- Fold several newspaper sheets into wedges. Put them in either the heels or the toes of your shoes to alter your centre of balance. You will tilt forwards or backwards, changing the way you move your arms and position your head as you walk.

QUICK-FIX WRINKLES

A great way to make yourself look older is by faking some wrinkles. Here's how to create the perfect look:

YOU WILL NEED

- flesh-coloured face paint, or foundation make-up
- pink or red face paint, or lipstick
- dark brown face paint, or eyeliner pencil
- white face paint, or white eyeliner pencil
- a thin paintbrush

1 Blend a little foundation or flesh-coloured face paint over your lips to cover them. Then repaint your lips to appear slightly thinner using the red or pink face paint, or lipstick.

2 Use the dark pencil or paint to draw a series of narrow vertical lines above your top lip and down into the corners of your mouth where creases form. Make sure you don't overdo the lines — experiment in front of a mirror until you get a convincing effect.

3 Wrinkle up your forehead and screw up your eyes to see where your face creases naturally. Again use the dark pencil or paint to draw thin lines that follow the natural creases. This will exaggerate them.

4 With a clean finger, gently blend the edges of the wrinkles you have drawn into your skin.

5 Using the white face paint, draw a thin line either side of each wrinkle and blend with a clean finger again. This will give a more convincing three-dimensional effect.

HOW TO ...
WRITE INVISIBLE MESSAGES

Spies always need to improvise, and, if you need to write a secret message in a hurry, don't panic. There's more than one way to put pen to paper privately.

HARD PRESSED

1. Write out a message on a pad of paper using a ball-point pen. Press down hard on the top sheet of paper.

2. Remove the sheet you wrote on and destroy it.

3. The sheet below will contain your hidden message. To a casual observer, it should appear blank, but if a fellow agent gently scribbles over it with soft pencil, the message will be revealed.

WAXING LYRICAL

1. Have a look around your house for candles. Look for ones that match the colour of the paper you're writing your message on — if you have white paper, you need a white candle.

2. If the candle is new, it will already have a pointed end. Just trim off the wick before you get started. If the candle has been used, cut off the top and rub it down so that you have a good writing point to use like a pen.

3. Write a decoy message in pen on one side to disguise your secret message. Turn the paper over and write your message with the candle — press firmly to leave enough wax behind.

4. To reveal the secret message, sprinkle pencil shavings across the paper, which will stick to the wax, or use a dark crayon to scribble over the piece of paper. The waxy writing will then mysteriously appear.

NEAT AS A PIN

There is a great way to send a message without writing anything at all. Intrigued? Here's how to do it:

1. Find a newspaper and a pin. Open the paper at a random page that has lots of text on it.

2. Working across the page from left to right, make tiny pinpricks under each letter in the paper, spelling out the words in the order that they appear in your message.

3. Fold the corner of the page down to mark it. Close the paper then transfer it to a fellow spy using a dead-letter drop (see pages 44-47).

4. If intercepted, the newspaper will look perfectly normal to an enemy agent. The person that wants to read the message, simply needs to hold the correct page up to a light to reveal which letters have holes beneath them.

5. The page must be destroyed immediately after decoding.

WETTER IS BETTER

1 Grab two pieces of paper and a bowl of cold water. Dip one sheet quickly into the water, remove it and lay it flat.

2 Lay the second, dry piece of paper over the wet one.

3 Use a pen or pencil to write your message on the dry, top sheet. Press as hard as you can without ripping the wet lower sheet, then destroy the top sheet.

4 At first you will be able to see your message on the damp sheet quite easily – don't worry.

5 Hang the wet paper over a radiator or on a clothes rack over the bath to dry. Alternatively, give it a quick blast with a hairdryer.

6 Once dry, pass the message on to a fellow agent.

7 To reveal the hidden writing, all your fellow spies need to do is to get the paper wet again.

HOW TO ...
BE A MORSE MASTER

Morse code has been around for over 180 years. It was originally invented by Samuel F. B. Morse in the United States and was used for military communications and radiotelegraphy. It is one of the simplest and most versatile codes around, and it's a great way for you and your fellow spies to signal to one another. This code can be written out, tapped out, or even flashed using torches.

The different combinations of dots, '•', or 'dits', and dashes '-', or 'dahs', are used to represent each letter of the alphabet. A dit should last the length of time it takes to say the word 'dit'. A dah should last three times longer than a dit.

The secret to mastering Morse is to get to grips with the difference between a dit, a dah and a break between words.

Once you've mastered the timing, you'll need to learn the Morse code alphabet, shown opposite.

`'...I.I.  -.--I---I..-`
`.-..I.-I-I.I.-.`
`.-I.--I.--I..I---I.-I-I-I---I.-.'`

MORSE CODE ALPHABET AND NUMBERS

A	·−	J	·−−−	S	···	2	··−−−
B	−···	K	−·−	T	−	3	···−−
C	−·−·	L	·−··	U	··−	4	····−
D	−··	M	−−	V	···−	5	·····
E	·	N	−·	W	·−−	6	−····
F	··−·	O	−−−	X	−··−	7	−−···
G	−−·	P	·−−·	Y	−·−−	8	−−−··
H	····	Q	−−·−	Z	−−··	9	−−−−·
I	··	R	·−·	1	·−−−−	0	−−−−−

To leave a break between words, say 'dit' to yourself five times. This will allow a long enough pause before you start the next word in your sentence.

Start off slowly at first — you'll be able to build up more speed the better you get.

Can you translate the message beside each picture below? Slashes have been used to clearly separate individual letters.

'··/−· ·− ·−−/····/···/·−−·/
−·−·/·−··/−−−/−·−·/−−−/−··/··/·−··/·'

Translation: In a while crocodile

CREATE A FAKE IDENTITY CARD

You're on a top-secret mission and need to gain access to a certain mysterious-looking building. When two suspicious-looking guards stop you, how will you manage to get past?

Simple — your own identity card. Here's how you can custom-make an ID card to suit any mission you might undertake.

YOU WILL NEED

- a passport photo of yourself (or of yourself in the disguise you're going to wear)
- a thin sheet of plain, white card
- scissors
- a computer (or a pen)
- some ink (preferably in a stamping pad
- a potato (yes, a potato)
- a small kitchen knife
- a pencil
- sticky-backed plastic

1   Cut a piece of paper to the size of a standard debit or credit card (ask to borrow one from an adult to get the measurements if you don't have your own cash card).

2   Stick your photo in the top right-hand corner of the paper.

3   Now add some details around your fake ID picture. You can do this with a pen if you're careful or on a computer for a more professional finish. Include a fake name, a fake ID number, phone number and the 'department' you work for.

4   At the top of the card, include your fake employer's name. If you're using a computer, design your own logo and paste it into your ID card. Why not pretend you're from a water or electricity company to give yourself a realistic, but vague excuse for being there?

5   Add a signature at the bottom of your fake ID — the less readable it is, the better.

6   Now you need to add an official-looking stamp in the bottom corner of the card. To do this, cut a potato in half with the knife and dab the cut end with some kitchen paper to soak up the juice. Now draw on a simple design using your pencil. Use the knife to cut away the background, leaving your design standing proud. Dip the potato into the ink and make sure the design is covered.

7   Firmly stamp the potato print onto your ID card and, once the ink is dry, cover the front and back of the card in sticky-backed plastic to give it a glossy finish.

If you have access to a computer, the perfect ID card will be even simpler to achieve. Work on your designs and build up a whole library of fake ID cards, so you can prepare yourself with one before every mission.

HOW TO ...

CREATE SECRET SIGNALS

AND SIGNPOSTS

If you're following a suspect and can't call for help, it's easy to leave a secret trail for your fellow agents to follow. Here are a few simple precautions to bear in mind:

- Plan a series of signs in advance to make sure that your fellow agents know what your signs mean.

- Use natural objects that you can find lying around, or use chalk to write signs that can easily be removed.

- Don't destroy or permanently mark any objects when you leave your trail.

- Don't over-use signs — the more you leave, the more likely they are to be spotted. So, only leave a sign if you have something important to point out.

- Place signs near the route but not on a path or where they might be disturbed or destroyed.

- If you're following a trail of signposts, always rub out or rearrange them as you move on so that no one else can follow them.

SECRET SIGNS

The signs you leave don't need to be complicated. They should be easy to leave, easy to remove and easy to understand. Here are some classic signs to get you started:

An arrow made from twigs: THIS WAY

A small stone in the middle of a larger stone: YOU'RE ON THE RIGHT TRAIL

A small stone to the left of a larger stone: TURN LEFT

A small stone to the right of a larger stone: TURN RIGHT

A circle of stones around a central stone:
GONE HOME / CANCEL TRAIL

A circle of stones around a
number of pebbles: SHOWS NUMBER OF
PACES YOU SHOULD WALK IN DIRECTION
OF ARROW TO FIND A MESSAGE

A cross made of twigs:
DON'T GO THIS WAY

A triangle made of twigs: WARNING

SEE EVERYTHING WITHOUT BEING SPOTTED

Make sure you get the best view of any suspicious activities, even if you're behind a wall or around a corner, with your very own periscope. Here's how:

YOU WILL NEED

- 2 cardboard juice cartons
- a marker pen • scissors
- a ruler • strong tape
- 2 flat mirrors, or mirrored card
- poster paints — various colours

1 Use the scissors to cut out a square opening at the bottom of one carton, as shown. Leave a centimetre frame around the sides and bottom of the opening for strength.

2 Place the carton on its side with the square opening towards you. Use your ruler to draw a diagonal line at a 45° angle, from the corner nearest the opening.

3 Cut along the line you have drawn. Slide the mirror into this slot. Check that you can see the top of the carton reflected in the mirror through the hole you've already made in the front. Then use the strong tape to fix the mirror in place.

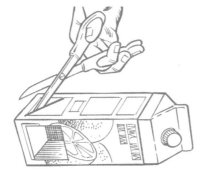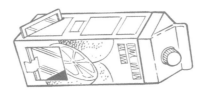

4 Repeat steps 1 to 3 with the other carton.

5 Carefully remove the roof-shaped tops from each carton with the scissors.

6 Position the cartons with their open ends together, with one mirror facing you and the other mirror facing in the opposite direction. Look at the mirror facing you. You should see the view from the other mirror reflected into it. Use the strong tape to join the cartons together.

7 Cover the juice cartons in poster paints to disguise them. You could use brown and green paints for a forest stakeout, sandy colours for desert reconnaissance, or shades of white and grey for surveillance in snowy conditions.

Your periscope is complete. Take it out and about for a test run. Use it upright to find out what's going on over a wall, or on its side to be the first to know who is coming around a corner.

HOW TO ...

MAKE A SPY RING BADGE

Badges are an essential part of a spy's equipment – they can be worn as subtle signals to other spies, with different badges having different meanings. You and your fellow agents should buy or make a number of badges with the same designs, so that each spy has a matching set.

Your set should include: one red, one green, one blue, one yellow, one with a star and one with a cross. You can get badge-making kits from craft shops and there are even websites where you can order your own badge designs.

Pin the badge to your clothes as usual and no one will suspect you are carrying a secret message.

1 In advance, you should all agree what each badge design means.

For example, you could use:

- a red badge to signal danger
- a green one to signal that all is clear
- a yellow one to signal that the spy ring needs to meet at base soon
- a blue badge to signal that you have a message to deliver.

2 Start by wearing the cross badge regularly, so people are used to you wearing them, and you don't arouse suspicions. The cross means that there is no message.

3 Choose the star badge as an 'identifier' — a secret way of identifying yourself as a member of the spy ring. This also enables you to spot other friendly spies without having to make contact with them.

4 When you need to send a signal, just pop on the most appropriate badge during your next mission.

Use a badge to carry secret messages — if you're in a hurry, badges can be used to hide messages that you don't want enemy agents to see. Fold the message up very small and wedge it in the back of the badge. For extra security, use a small amount of sticky tape to keep it in place or pierce it with the badge pin.

HOW TO ...
MOUNT AN UNDERSEA RESCUE

You're on a mission to infiltrate the underwater HQ of an international criminal mastermind. You and your fellow agent must scuba dive through the secret underwater entrance to the cave in order to take the enemy by surprise.

WARNING:

Before attempting any kind of a scuba-diving rescue in the real world, seek training with a qualified instructor — or you may find you need rescuing yourself.

Once you have safety checked your diving gear and put it on, fall back into the sea, holding your mask and snorkel to your face. Wait for the cloud of bubbles to clear. Give your fellow agent the 'okay' signal (see page 53) and kick down to the reef. A shoal of fish flashes silver as you swim past. You spot the entrance to the cave less than 50 m away.

Suddenly, you realize that your companion has stopped swimming. They are waving frantically at you – something has gone wrong and they are suddenly out of air! You'll need to share your air supply. Here's what to do:

1 Swim over and hold on to your partner's jacket with your left hand.

2 Take a deep breath and then calmly remove the regulator (mouthpiece) from your mouth.

3 Push the button on the regulator to clear it of water and then hand it to your buddy. Hold up three fingers to tell them to take three breaths.

4 When they have finished and hand back the regulator, clear it again as you did before. Do this at every exchange.

5 Continue to hold on to each other and breathe in this way until you have established a rhythm and your companion has calmed down.

6 When you are both ready, give a thumbs up to signal you are heading back up to the surface. Lead the ascent and swim upwards at a steady rate, at a speed no faster than your bubbles.

7 When you break the surface, head straight back to the support boat. Report back to base and return to the safe house on shore. Your mission has just been postponed.

USE A WALKIE-TALKIE

If you're lucky enough to have a walkie-talkie set,
you'll know what a great piece of equipment it is,
making it easier for you to stay in touch
whenever you're on a mission.

ROGER, ROGER?

To sound like a professional radio operator, you'll need to use proper 'voice procedure'. Here's what you should say and when to say it:

- 'Roger' for 'message received'
- 'Copy' for 'message is understood'
- 'Wilco' for 'will comply' — you're going to follow the instructions
- 'Say again' for 'repeat message'
- 'Over' to say, 'my message is complete, waiting for a response'
- 'Out' to say that the conversation is complete.

Use the sound of your voice to indicate whether or not you are asking a question, or making a statement. For example, if you say 'Copy', it sounds as though you have understood the other agent's message. If you say 'Copy?' they will know that you are asking if they have understood your message.

It's also very easy for anyone nearby to listen in and overhear what you're saying ... unless you can confuse communications with the '10' code system.

Police forces use '10' codes to keep conversations over the radio as short as possible. You can use the same system, or develop your own version, so that only you and your fellow agents know what you are talking about.

SOME STARTERS FOR 'TEN'

Here are some useful phrases from the '10'-code system to get you started. Get together with everyone in your spy ring and memorize this code:

- '10-1' means 'I can't hear you'
- '10-2' means 'I can hear you loud and clear'
- '10-3' means 'stop speaking'
- '10-4' means 'message understood'
- '10-5 (plus name)' means 'pass message to (plus name)'
- '10-6' means 'please repeat what you said'
- '10-7' means 'no'
- '10-8' means 'stand by for a message'
- '10-9' means 'other people are present and listening'
- '10-10' means 'urgent, help needed'
- '10-11' means 'return to base'
- '10-12' means 'where are you?'
- '10-12 (plus location)' means 'I am in (plus location)'
- '10-13' means 'abandon operation'
- '10-14' means 'false alarm', or 'all clear'.

HOW TO ...

USE A CODE BOOK

Books aren't just useful for learning spycraft skills or for hiding mirrors on surveillance missions (see pages 64-65), they can also be used to create a highly-secure code.

1. All the spies in your ring need to buy exactly the same edition of a book. You can choose any book you want, although it's a good idea to get one that is quite long (200-300 pages) so that it has plenty of words in it. This will be your code book.

2. When writing a secret message to your fellow spies you'll need to identify the page number, the line number, and the number of words along the line that each word appears. Everyone should agree in which order you will encode these to pinpoint specific words in the book, such as 'page – line – word'.

For example, if the first word in your coded message is 'meet', flick through your code book until you find this word in it. If the word 'meet' appears on page 12, that will be the first part of your code: '12'. Then to narrow down the search for this word identify which line the word is on, counting down from the top of the page. If 'meet' is on line 15 of page 12 your code would read: '12 – 15'. The final piece of information your fellow spies need is how far along the line to look. Assuming that 'meet' is the third word along from the left, you should then add this number to the code you have already written: '12 – 15 – 3'.

3. Write out the code for each word of your message in a column of numbers. Only your fellow spies, who know exactly which book to use to decode it, will understand what you have written.

You can also receive similarly encoded messages in return. As long as the identity of your code book remains secret, it should be almost impossible for anyone else to crack your code and decipher your communications.

115 – 14 – 6? (Use this book to decode that message!)

HOW TO ...

CRACK A CODE

Once you have learned to make all the codes in this book, you will already be one step closer to knowing how to crack any coded messages you might intercept from rival agents. A substitution code (see page 49) is the easiest to practise breaking. To help you on the way, here are some tricks to try to become a killer code-cracker.

1 Look for any repeated letters or sequences of letters. Any recurring pattern will help you to identify the type of code that has been used.

2 Try swapping the first and last letters of words in the code in case any obvious solutions jump out at you.

3 Check what happens if you write the message out backwards – you may spot some words you recognize.

4 Look out for the most common symbol or letter that appears in the message. In the English language the most common letter is 'E', so that letter in your message is almost certainly an 'E'. Try to work out if there is a pattern between the code version of 'E' and the letter 'E'. For example, if the letter 'E' appears as an 'F' every time in the message, it would suggests that code has been made by replacing each letter with the one next to it in the alphabet.

5 As soon as you find a letter you have decoded, write it in capitals under the symbol or coded letter.

6 Look out for any short words that could be 'to', 'and', 'at', 'I' or 'a'. The most common three-letter word in English is 'the'. If you recognize an 'E' at the end of a three letter word, write 'T' and 'H' below the corresponding letters.

7 Slowly build up the number of letters you think you can decode. Once you have two or three, you may be able to start guessing at more words. If you have decoded two letters either side of another, take an educated guess at what it might be. Then see what happens if you write the decoded letter under the coded version in other places.

8 Look for patterns in words. If you decode a 'Q', it's almost certain the next letter is 'U'. 'H' often follows 'C' and so on.

9 Don't be afraid to experiment and get things wrong, but as soon as you decode a letter, keep thinking about how it could unlock the entire code.

10 Don't give up. Once you work out two or three letters, you should have enough to crack any substitution code.

DECRYPTION TEST

Write out a copy of these coded messages for each of your recruits. Get them to try out their code-breaking skills, using the methods described here. Give two points for each code they break, one point if they need a clue, and none if they flunk out completely. Clues and solutions are on page 123. Record their results using the chart template on page 127.

1. Qeb pmv jxpqbo fp lrqpqxkafkd.

2. Ztte je iwt vdds ldgz, ndj'gt vtiixcv qtiitg paa iwt ixbt.

3. Svzwjfzigvih szh yvvm rmezwvw – wl mlg zkkilzxs.

4. Rednfiltratei neeber sahed ginred reyps ruore.

5. Maxx buva, kuo era vum e weqpar cuba-draeyar.

HOW TO SOLVE THE DECRYPTION TEST

If you or your agents need extra help with the test on page 122, here are some clues to point you in the right direction.

1. If 'B' is 'E', what might 'X' be? Try writing the alphabet out and replacing these letters.

The spy master is outstanding.

2. Which letter might 'T' be? It is a very popular letter. Write the alphabet out again and try a substitution code.

Keep up the good work, you're getting better all the time.

3. What would happen if you reversed the alphabet? Try starting switching 'A' with 'Z' and working backwards.

Headquarters has been invaded — do not approach.

4. Remember the Swap-Shop code on page 51? Apply those rules to this code to discover this important warning.

Our spy ring has been infiltrated.

5. If you make the code wheel on pages 76-79 you'll be the code-breaking king!.

Well done, you are now a master code-breaker.

AN A-Z OF SPY SPEAK

Use this glossary to make sure you know all the specific spycraft terminology you need to be the best spy ever.

AGENT – a spy

CALL SIGN – radio code name

CAMOUFLAGE – disguising yourself or an object to hide it

CIPHER – a code

CODE NAME – your secret 'spy name'

CONTACT – the person you speak to about a mission

DEAD-LETTER DROP – the place you leave your messages for other spies

DEBRIEFING – discussing the mission when it has finished

DECIPHER – to break a code

DOSSIER – your documents about a mission

DOUBLE AGENT – an agent secretly working for the enemy

ENCODING/ENCRYPTION – to conceal a message in a code

ESPIONAGE – spying

FIELD AGENT – a spy who goes on missions

GO-BETWEEN – the contact between field agents and the spy master

HQ – short for headquarters

INCOGNITO – hiding your real identity

INFILTRATE – sneakily gain access to another spy ring

INTELLIGENCE – information on your mission or target

MARK – the target you are following

OPERATION – the spy ring's mission or plan

RECCE – short for reconnaissance mission

RENDEZVOUS – a meeting with another spy

SHADOW – the spy following you

SPY MASTER – the person in charge of the spy ring

SPY RING – a group of spies working together

SURVEILLANCE – observation of a particular target or mark

TAIL – follow another spy

TARGET – the person you need to follow

UNFRIENDLIES – enemies

HOW TO ...

TRAIN A NEW RECRUIT

Throughout this book there are some useful tests that you can use to monitor your recruits' core spying abilities, as well as your own.

Get each recruit to make a copy of the chart opposite to record their scores. They should fill it in using their code names (see page 29) with marks out of ten for each test.

Make a record of their progress to see how they improve over time. Remember, just because a recruit starts off badly in some areas, this does not mean they won't make a useful team member in many other ways.

CODE NAME: ....

TEST	SCORE OUT OF TEN
Memory test one (page 37)	☐
Memory test two (page 39)	☐
Memory test three (page 39)	☐
Code-breaking (page 122)	☐

CONGRATULATIONS

THIS IS TO CERTIFY THAT

. . . .

IS NOW A

BUSTER KNOW-HOW EXPERT